HAVE YOU BEEN FEELING BLUE THESE DAYS?
요즘 우울하십니까?

KIM EON HEE

김언희

TRANSLATED BY SUNG GI KIM & EUNSONG KIM

HAVE YOU BEEN FEELING BLUE THESE DAYS?
요즘 우울하십니까?

KIM EON HEE
김언희

TRANSLATED BY SUNG GI KIM & EUNSONG KIM

Copyright © 2019 Sung Gi Kim & Eunsong Kim

Book Cover & Interior Design: Sarah Gzemski

Published with support from LTI Korea

LTI Korea

Published by Noemi Press, Inc. A Nonprofit Literary Organization.
www.noemipress.org.

CONTENTS INSIDE

Foreword from the Translators — 9
시인의 말 — 15

I

Thunderstruck Kiss	벼락 키스	21
Salmon	연어	22
Happy Sunday	해피 선데이	23
As Soon as I Bite the Mouth Gag	개구기(開口期)를 물자 말자	24
A Morning opened by Poetry	시로 여는 아침	25
Without		26
없소		27
		28
This Night	이 밤	29
Stage Direction 104	지문104	30
The Reason Blood Doesn't Circulate through the Brain	머리에 피가 안도는 이유	31
Situation D	정황 D	32
I Have Endured		33
나는 참아주었네		34
Bird,	새는,	35
9999 9999 9999	9999 9999 9999	36
A List of Chronic Diseases	지병의 목록	37
Emperor Squid	대왕오징어	38
Have You Been Feeling Blue These Days?	요즘 우울하십까?	39
A Bubble's Birth 1	거품의 탄생 1	40
A Seashore's Tomb	해변의 묘지	41
EX. 1) Carefully read the answers on the next page, and create proper questions out of your answers. (Describe in short answer form)		42
EX. 1) 옆 페이지의 정답을 잘 읽고, 그 정답에 적절한 질문을 작성하시오 (주관식 서술형)		44
Jangchung's King-size Pork Feet	장충왕족발	46
Those Cats!	저 고양이들!	47

Star-Shining-Night	별이 빛나는 밤	48
Just a Moment	잠시	49

II

Vaseline Symphony	바셀린 심포니	55
Ark	방주(方舟)	56
Even Now Something	아직도 무엇이	57
Habituation (習)		58
습(習)		59
		60
EX. 2) The insides ( ) of the poem below can be newly filled accordingly to your unique preferences		
	EX. 2) 아래 시는 ( )속에 여러분의 취향에 맞는 낱말을 넣어 새로 쓸 수 있습니다	61
Mantra	만트라	62
The Traveler at the Beach	해변의 길손	63
Vexations	벡사시옹(Vexations)	64
Don't You Know When You Go You End up Sitting Down	가게 되면 앉게 되거든	66
Feeding the Moon	달에게 먹이다	67
Funeral Bumper Car		68
운구(運柩)용 범퍼 카		69
Your Mouth	너의 입	70
Playing With Fireworks on the Moon 1	달나라의 불장난 1	71
Playing With Fireworks on the Moon 2	달나라의 불장난 2	72
Summer Icicle	여름 고드름	73
Day of Mourning	기(忌)	74
After We Have Loved	사랑한 뒤에는	75
Before You Came	네가 오기 전	76
Rodeo	로데오	77
Postscript	추신	78
A Very Special Bouquet	아주 특별한 꽃다발	79
Magna Carta	마그나 카르타	80

III

Bruise	멍	85
Plum	자두	86
Together	더불어	87
Fish Cake Dumplings	완자 어육(魚肉)	89
Snuff, Snuff, Snuff		90
스너프, 스너프, 스너프		91
Liaison		92
밀통(密通)		93
Mantis	사마귀	94
The Portrait of Princess Bonaparte	보나파르트 공주의 초상	95
Someone, Again	누가, 또	96
A Very Very Blue Meridian	아주아주 푸른 자오선	97
Shadow Spider (Yaginumia Sia)	그늘왕거미	98
A Bubble's Birth 2	거품의 탄생 2	99
Her Specialty, Doorbell	십팔번, 요비링	100
Her Specialty, Foxtail	십팔번, 낭미초(狼尾草)	101
Prelude	프렐류드	102
Buck Teeth	뻐드렁니	103
(Whisperingly)		104
(속삭이듯이)		105
5 Minutes Have Passed	5분이 지났다	106
Pieta Signore	피에타 시뇨레	107
Ver. 1 Ignite	Ver.1. 발화	108
Filthy Love	사련(邪戀)	109
The Dragon Door's Aftertaste	용문(龍門)의 뒷맛	110
Returning Home	환향	111
Epilogue	에필로그	112
Acknowledgements		115

FOREWORD FROM THE TRANSLATORS

In 1932, at the start of his exile from what would become Hitler's Third Reich, the German Jewish philosopher Walter Benjamin suggested that, rather than insisting on the absolute originality of a particular language and romanticizing the impossibility of translation, that we think of translation instead as "[serving] the purpose of expressing the central reciprocal relationship between languages." "Languages," he wrote, "are not strangers to one another, but are, a priori and apart from all historical relationships, interrelated in what they want to express[1]." And we agree. Addressing the reciprocity and interrelations between language systems and their attendant political structures—here between Korean and English—cannot help but be illuminating for any examination of the neo-colonial, neo-liberal world order.

In the realm of popular representations, South Korea continues to be touted as an economic miracle: it suffered inter-imperial war in relative anonymity, it reproduced the social structures laid out during the history of colonization, it adopted American capitalism as its secular religion.

But SK tests certain limits of global capitalist expansion, as K-pop, K-beauty, K-film, and even the Hangeul alphabet circulate as mass consumer products[2]. Consider SK's never-ending appetite for free trade agreements. Consider too SK's emergence as the world's largest weapons importer in 2014, a notorious title held by the United States until then. Relationship: The US has remained the single largest weapons exporter since 1950. The postwar US consumes itself in and as a cache

---

[1] Walter Benjamin, "The Task of the Translator" from *Illuminations*, trans. Harry Zohn; ed. & intro. Hannah Arendt. New York: Harcourt Brace Jovanovich 1968.
[2] For more on this see, "South Korea's entertainment industry is part of what's known as "Hallyu" or "The Korean Wave." CGTN October 3rd, 2018. And "Asian Idol Industries: South Korea sees soft power opportunity, as neighbors mimic K-pop's business model," CGTN October 4th, 2018.

of armaments to protect *whiteness as property*[3]. Consider that K-pop dance routines are exported across South East Asia as an act of governmental "service." Consider too the lawsuits filed by SK corporations in Cambodia, Burma, and China against garment workers for protesting exploitation and repression.

South Korea's positioning, increasingly, as a neo-colonial neo-colonizer, a mercenary state—as poet Don Mee Choi has described it—can be witnessed in the ways its prized cultural products of export move in direct contradiction to the aesthetics necessary for survival. The convoluted relationship thus forged between Korean & English: economic and political collaborators in the neo-liberalization of the world. And?

So what can poetry, particularly the translation of Korean language poetry, be or become under such conditions?

*

Kim Eon Hee (b. 1953) is a self-taught poet residing in Jinju, Korea. Her first collection, *Modern Ars Poetica* was published in 1989, and this collection *Have You Been Feeling Blue These Days?* her fourth collection was first published in 2011. She has published over 5 volumes of poetry, and has been organizing community poetry groups out of Jinju for 30 years.

Kim began the poetry group as a way to support herself and her community. Of the collective she notes that though prominent poets have emerged from their meetings, such as Kim Yideum and Yoo Hong Jun, the premise to begin the group was and is the fostering of a non-antagonistic poetic space for anyone interested. In particular Kim notes how, "Not everyone can take poetry classes, particularly the socio-econom-

---

[3] Harris, Cheryl. "Whiteness as Property." Harvard Law Review. 106.8 (Jun., 1993): 1707-1791

ically disadvantaged." And that, "I started this group because when I started writing I endured loops and holes. It was miserable. And I wanted others not to have to endure that." She then clarifies how she positions her politics, which she defines as anarchist: "On the side of the weak."

Kim tells us that, "In the past, I was weak and right and in the future I remain weak. In the past, I was weak because I was weak.... In the future, I am weak because I am dead. As a poet, I am an outsider of Korean culture (that is why I am weak). I am someone who has nothing left to lose. Which also makes me the strongest."

This sentiment can be traced throughout Kim's poetry, which is contradictory, complex, unafraid of graphic disappointment, the pits. In her introduction, she writes that she wants this collection to be, "Poetry that tears the paper: that kind of excellence. I wanted this to be so good that you could not forgive me." Her poetry is as playful as it is stark, as ambivalent as it politically charged. Is this poetry another relationship betwixt Korean and English? The positioning of poetry, somewhere below and weak, somewhere easy and disregarded or too sacred and elsewhere? As the last export frontier?

As an unexpectedly politicized space?

*

In the official relationship between Korean and English, Korean is classified as an isolate language — meaning there is currently no discernible linguistic lineage. English is classified as a West Germanic language, with infusions from the Romance languages. The relationship is so systematically disconnected that it has required inventions: third person gender pronouns in Korean, for instance, to accommodate English translations[4]. Politically, everything has been made possible.

We found Kim Eon Hee's poetry during a cultural and economic moment in which K-poetry became "trendy." People with little to no knowledge of Korean, Korean history, with no ties to its literary and political traditions have become translators and consumers of Korean poetry. How?

We can already feel the energies that will be marshaled in service of a response. It has been explained to us, formally and informally, from multiple points along the spectrum, that translation and consumption have moved past linguistic knowledge per se. One does not need to know the non-western language to translate it into a western language (but don't dare consider attempting such the other way round). One only needs enthusiasm and desire whatever that may be.

Benjamin predicted this confusion: "Fidelity and freedom have traditionally been regarded as conflicting tendencies. This deeper interpretation of the one apparently does not serve to reconcile the two; in fact, it seems to deny the other all justification. For what is meant by freedom but that the rendering of the sense is no longer to be regarded as all important?" So without spiraling into an uninteresting and shopworn debate regarding authenticity, accuracy, and the politics of aptitude and freedom—we care for none of that—we do think it's vital to discuss authority as it relates to knowledge.

In translating Kim Eon Hee's poetry, our Korean was pushed, tested; our English ever more fragmented. We realized that we knew less than we believed—which is not an occasion for celebrating and justifying

---

[4]See Krista Ryu's "Gender distinction in languages." *Language Log* Oct 2017.

our mistakes—but reminders that countered what began as our self-assured authority.

What we offer here are not translations, but another relationship between Korean and English.

What is here is the semblance of a feeling that we hope you know we can witness only outside of language.

What we have labored through is the acceptance of this distance, and the hope of its portending something else.

*

Last note of importance regarding relationships: Though this is our first translated collection, we have been forever translating. Like so many mundane immigration narratives, we grew up translating and interpreting for our family members. Our mother in particular refused English. She refused it in public. At home. At church. She refused her language lessons. Our father would enroll her in community college courses and she would demand that he do her homework. She then stopped going to the classes.

We called all the operators. We started by telling them the truth. One of us would say: Hello, I am the daughter of xyz and I am calling to interpret for her. Hello, I am the son of so and so and I calling to interpret for her. The operators would respond aggressively, suspiciously—sometimes they would demand: how old are you? The number of security questionnaires piled high, so we just started stating: Hello I'm xyz, I'm calling about my phone service. You over billed us. Again.

This an ordinary story that fits many. Growing up as the interpreter, as the translator means you run twice as many errands. It means you sit through all their meetings. It means the gossip you overhear is multi-generational. Because our parents worked in a church, we overheard everyone's secrets. Did you know he's having an affair with abc? But she doesn't know! This is where their money comes from. Etc.

Our mother, other than refusing this dialect and idiom, refused driving. The two things often demanded of subjects in the United States, she said: No. She hated the activity overall but driving home one day, a white man rear-ended her car. When she got out to address the scene and he realized her hesitation in responding to him, he called a friend to drive over and act as a witness. And then he called the police. His friend, the "witness," told the police officer that our mother was recklessly driving and suddenly stopped, so yeah maybe the guy rear-ended her but it's not his fault. At the very least it's both of their faults. It's her fault for not speaking English, and it's his fault for rear-ending her. This formula equals it is both of their faults. And my mother said: Fuck this, not in English, and stopped driving altogether.

*

Since our parents have immigrated back to the motherland, our interpretation and translation requests have all but disappeared. Now, at the request of no one, we interpret the power dynamics that structure our relationships and translate their ethical stakes.

We consider this book to be the first public extension of this new project.

—Sung Gi Kim, Eunsong Kim 2019

시인의 말

책을 끝내는 것은 아이를 뒤뜰로 데려 가 총으로 쏴 버리는 것과 같아, 카포티가 말했습니다. 은둔자는 늙어 가면서 악마가 되지, 뒤샹이 말했습니다. 웃다가 죽은 해골들은 웃어서 죽음을 미치게 한다네, 내가 말했습니다.

종이가 찢어질 정도로 훌륭한 시를, 용서할 수 없을 정도로 잘 쓰고 싶었습니다

2011년 이 시집을 읽어 주시는 분들께
김언희

I

Thunderstruck Kiss

While being thunderstruck

I wonder, what is the tree doing

As lightning enters into the mouth

It thrashes through the womb

Exiting after penetration

Laying mouth to mouth with the thunderbolts

Salmon

Once a day they flippantly lay twenty thousand eggs, salmon

Returning only to swallow their twenty thousand eggs, salmon

Twenty thousand shudders made daily, salmon

From now on won't do it with no one, salmon

Everyone's incesting be it Mr. Kim or Mr. Park, salmon

All the ass holes are mixed with blood, salmon

Happy Sunday

The lions in the animal factory
Cover their whole bodies with elephant shit
Massaging themselves and smiling

Sunday

After the tithes are received
God
Decadently
Ingests
My sins

When you call out
Honey!
All the neighborhood dogs
Look around

Kind of Sunday

Lover for my lover
To be laid kind of Sunday
Lover above the lover
The accumulation

Sunday

As Soon as I Bite the Mouth Gag

As soon I bite the mouth gag, I wanna eat dog meat. *It's rotten to the root. The rotten gums,* the rotting shame, *can't be numbed.* How are you all dead but say the rotten one is me! The treacherous, treachery-ful Jordan river is really only messy ditch water.

Jordan, you're my dog! The maw that's been slurping the moth
balls in the closet, with that maw please slurp my toes.
Please suck them, treacherous dog. Though your teeth have
completely fallen out for biting something so scalding!

In a dream, *did that girl go till the end with the first guy, did they love until the anchovies could be peeled? Are they removing the innards together till the end?* Charlton Heston asked, in the dream. Naked with only a raincoat hanging. His butt was like a block of ice, I've never

Never have been a cherry Miss Cherry. Of all places,
How did
A mouth appear here. Of all places how did teeth sprout up
With this mouth I obsessively loved! Chop chop chop like a dog
Chewing bones.

A Morning Opened by Poetry

Honey let's read the poem on the toilet

Even on mornings when the white hairs can't be tweezed

However first let's read the poem on the toilet

Before checking the texture of the bowel movements at the start of the day

May it be a thin thick long short shit, before the start of the day

Putting on a solemn complexion, put on a solemn complexion honey

We shit in the same spot more than a thousand times

Dearest your face is like a dam ready to burst

Through the grandeur afforded by not writing poems now I know no I know

Without

There is no such thing as an agave-like thing here no such thing as a broken jaw bone-like thing no such half alive cat-like thing no such voluptuous spider-like thing spider monkey-like thing no such coming down backwards crawling-like thing no such mother-like thing no such thing as a loving mother smiling like a rotting pear rotten coal black pear-like thing no such thickened artificial waterfall-like thing no such god-like thing public toilet lever thing here no such rat-like skewered by the umbrella stem-like thing no such dead of the night shaving blue in the dead of the night shaving the flat of the tongue-like thing no such scream howl-like thing no such floor-like thing specter-like thing before the child could be the dead child-like thing that poem-like thing no such things are here no such blue child spinning in the blue dish-like thing like when a swarm of bees whimpers of death like when a swarm of bees tangle and tangle with death until the flesh becomes gold like ripening apricots like stair-like things such stair-like things no such things are here

없소

용설란 같은 것은 여기에 없소 깨어진 턱뼈 같은 것은 여기에 없소 설죽은 고양이 같은 것은 여기에 없소 요염한 거미 같은 것은 거미원숭이 같은 것은 여기에 없소 거꾸로 기어 내려 올 벽 같은 것은 여기에 없소 어머니 같은 것은 여기에 없소 사랑하는 어머니 썩은 배처럼 웃으시는 썩은 배 시커멓게 썩은 배 같은 것은 여기에 없소 걸쭉한 인공 폭포 같은 것은 여기에 없소 하느님 같은 것은 공중 변기 레버 같은 것은 여기에 없소 우산대에 꿰인 쥐 같은 것은 여기 없소 심야의 면도질 새파랗게 면도질한 혓바닥 같은 것은 여기에 없소 비명 같은 것은 바닥 같은 것은 유령 같은 것은 여기에 없소 생기기도 전에 죽은 아이 같은 것은 시 같은 것은 여기에 없소 파란 아이가 돌리는 파란 접시 같은 것은 여기에 없소 벌떼처럼 죽음이 잉잉거리고 벌떼처럼 죽음이 꼬이고 꼬이고 다만 살이 금이 되도록 익는 살구 계단 같은 것 계단 같은 것은 여기에 없소

This Night

There are corpses dangling from the colonnade of trees
No one is watching
Not even the Siamese twins
And it's not even special anymore

If they line me up and feed me shit
I will line up in a single file to eat shit, singing the national anthem
How can this indigenous song be playing, when we're catching the skunk,
After 10 years the gloves used back then
Still reek

My life
Is a promotional trial event
I am the type of giveaway
Even dogs would laugh at

You know we came this far by slipping on the banana peel
It was because
Whether we slipped on the banana peel
On the first night
Or the last night
Neither here nor there
Can't even be this night

The moment it goes in can't actually be put in,
The moment of death can't actually die this night

Stage Direction 104

Your role is the chair, used on the stage as a substitute for a tomb
You know, a chair?
The people who sit on the chair are the people who have all died or
Are the characters considered to be dead

Of course you don't have any lines, and the characters sit and die, they're still
And will rot, of course they'll sit on top of you
The rocking chair of death, because
You are the final resting chair

Even though your role is the chair, you are the protagonist
The characters are props
Like black taffy discharge that spills they rot sitting on top of you
They are like fatal props

You enter with four legs and naturally you walk out with four

To adjust your height
Sometimes the characters will step on your chin
Like they do to the pedal of a salon chair

The Reason Blood Doesn't Circulate through the Brain

The reason blood doesn't circulate through the brain
The reason to apply Preparation H on your lips
The reason dutiful hands desperately come out when searching for scissors
The reason you believe your sight has gone even though you're so clearly looking
The reason you can't do it on this bed anymore
And the reason size isn't the problem, rather
The reason you don't know the precise formula for the scope of deep-rooted sorrow, that kind of shit
So why even bother
The reason a sin committed by all is not a sin
The reason you can't say where you're going even though you've gotten into a taxi
The reason you do the same shit whether it's to die or to live
The reason dozens of years pass in between the question and answer
The reason you have to live until you don't know what is what
The reason you need a key to take a shit
And though you sweetly endlessly smile the reason luck doesn't come
The reason it won't come, like the rest
The reason your own bed becomes a foreign death bed away from home
The reason your dead mother desperately chases you
And why you end up only meeting her on a log bridge
The reason for being in the second grade for 40 years
The reason your poetry blows your nose

Situation D

I started menopause
At 12, I was told
To lay a spider web below my hole, if you're penetrated
There everything rots
And becomes decay, my
Hell, was my
Gutter, as I was asleep on the bed
In the deep blue sphagnum moss tub
I continued to awake, whether to cry
Or whether to laugh
I don't know where to put myself
During all crucial moments
My batteries die, I binge-eat dry rice
Till my eyes go blind, the gust tumbled a hat
And I chased it, till my two eyes
Go blind, but I laugh off
Everything
This laugh
Gives me goosebumps, even in August
I could see my breath, even to the aberration
I was an aberration, unapproachable
Bad breath
Radiating,

I Have Endured

I endured for, the morning breath I'm met with, endured for the unexpected touch, I endure feminism and, endure humanism and, I have endured intersectional relationships, I have endured the good poem of the **day**, the **day** there's no need to die or live, I have endured, 10 years worth of previously written diary entries, 100 years worth of transcribed financial records, I have endured the middle of the night fee increase, endured the broad daylight surcharge, for 30 years those all-night Friday prayers, for 30 years those all-night Friday fucks, I endured like a stray dog, whether backdoor dealing or underhanded dealings I endured laid out covered in newspapers, only for a life that's entirely to rot, the smell of my rotten flesh, I have endured, the lump of cement twisted and stuck on the rusting rebar, endured this shape this state, the constant street piss, endured the piss in my face, I endured the enduring me, starting fresh mornings always with a fresh lie, the spring breeze awakening some old horse dick,

나는 참아주었네

나는 참아 주었네, 아침에 맡는 입 냄새를, 뜻밖의 감촉을 참아 주었네, 페미니즘을 참아 주고, 휴머니즘을 참아 주고, 불가분의 관계를 참아 주었네, 나는 참아 주었네, 오늘의 좋은 시를, 죽을 필요도 살 필요도 없는 오늘을, 참아 주었네, 미리 써 놓은 십년 치의 일기를, 미리 써 놓은 백년 치의 가계부를, 참아 주었네, 한밤중의 수수료 인상을, 대낮의 심야 할증을 참아 주었네 나는, 금요일 철야기도 30년을, 금요일 철야 섹스 30년을, 주인 없는 개처럼 참아 주었네, 뒷거래도 밑 거래도 신문지를 깔고 덮고 참아 주었네, 오로지 썩는 것이 전부인 생을, 내 고기 썩는 냄새를, 나는 참아 주었네, 녹슨 철근에 엉겨 붙은 시멘트 덩어리를, 이 모양 이 꼴을 참아 주었네, 노상 방뇨를 참아 주었네, 면상 방뇨를 참아 주었네, 참는 나를 나는 참아 주었네, 늘 새로운 거짓말로 시작되는 새로운 아침을, 봄바람에 갈라 터지는 늙은 말 좆을,

Bird,

Even as the bird flies it shits, even as it shits it flies, *oh! oh! flung wide open and soaring into the vastness!* whether to expose the chin or not, from the corner's end, to the end, you sly sly while soaring you sly sly to defecate, wings and feces at the same time in the same motion, oh oh, the bird doesn't know constipation and doesn't know why there's bloody excrement and, doesn't know anal fistula and, doesn't know hemorrhoids, and the bird's head clank clank is empty and, to the bone clank clank as it rings it empties, oh oh, the bird shits even as it flies,

9999 9999 9999

The ducks that ordered the group to be buried alive
Had them resurrected

As the resurrected ducks stride
They shit fluorescent shit

Shit-stained duck head shit-stained duck head Andre Park
Wore a red petticoat and eagerly followed
Moving one step forward
Then trying to go three steps at a time
Going backwards instead

If
the earth is left in ruins tomorrow
Why wouldn't you be able to plant
The apple tree, why not
Or even thousands of them

My eyes are
Above the one white above the two black, truthfully
Is what you had to cover the leaves with
Your penis
Is it not?

Duckheadshitstainedduckheadshitstained

Every time you pull your hand out of your pocket it's
Smeared in shit so if you don't have
Pockets
Would there really be
No place for your hands to be?

A List of Chronic Diseases

The disease that returns home each day
Loses-its-way-in-the-living-room disease
Don't-know-why-I'm-here disease
Chatting-with-the-dead-in-the-middle-of-the-night disease
Reciting-a-quintet-by-myself disease
Wetting-myself-when-reading-an-exquisite-poem disease
Looking-outside-the-window-every-three-minutes disease
Vomiting-whenever-you-see-your-lover disease
Offering-whatever-I-bite disease
Day-by-day-gaining-confidence-from-my-stench disease
tightly-grasping-a-barely-hard-dick-to-go-write-a-poem disease
Stroking-the-nonexistent-balls disease
Smiling-wide-open-through-the-asshole disease
Spitting-out-saliva-with-my-eyes disease
To-endure-an-unbearable-comedy-till-the-end-to-endure-by-watching-it-till-the-end disease
To-intensively-wonder-how-I-could-be-the girl-the-masses-all-want-to-sleep-with disease
The spotlight that illuminates and displays your life's genitals disease
At-3-o'clock-filling-my-intestines-with-glass-noodles disease
Calling-god-'darling, darling' disease
Humming-at-the-stairwell-of-a-mortuary disease
Preemptively-taking-a-bitch-slap-for-an-action-you-may-not-do disease
Even-dogs-ask-if-they-can-eat-me-whenever-we-meet disease
Didn't-even-know-yesterday
Just-figuring-out-today disease

Emperor Squid

Grab the
Two ears
To be **suddenly** lifted

Should we just kiss
Cuz we're bored?

a sudden moment of the night like thick cum

I frantically grasp the emperor squid's two slippery earflaps

A thing no one has done
Should we do it, should we do it
Us, once?

The thing no one has swallowed, should we swallow it, once?

a sudden moment
of the night like cloudy cum

Have You Been Feeling Blue These Days?

Have you been feeling blue these days?
Are you struggling because of money?
Did you watch the viral videos?
Is this your castle in the sky?
Do your enemies appear as your parents?
Are you afraid of becoming an arsonist?
Do you want to suffer more from your sense of guilt?
Are you anxious you might step on a dead person's foot, somewhere?
Even though you're alone are you really not alone?
Do even dogs or cows belittle you?
Is your eye twitching and is pus pouring
Out of your gums?
Is smoke coming out from your asshole or ear hole?
Do your words come out like mushed rotten strawberries?
Are both your hands fool's gold, one holding amnesia and the other delirium?
Are you boundless and trapped? Suffocating and
In pitch-black? You'll likely go crazy soon
But like, only like
Are you like that?

Then please do click
Here

요즘 우울하십니까?

요즘 우울하십니까?
돈 때문에 힘드십니까?
문제의 동영상을 보셨습니까?
그림의 떡이십니까?
원수가 부모로 보이십니까?
방화범이 될까 봐 두려우십니까?
더 많은 죄의식에 시달리고 싶으십니까?
어디서 죽은 사람의 발등을 밟게 될 지 불안하십니까?
혼자 있어도 혼자 있는 게 아니십니까?
개나 소나 당신을 우습게봅니까?
눈 밑이 실룩거리고 잇몸에서
고름이 흘러내리십니까?
밑구멍이나 귀구멍에서 연기가 흘러나오십니까?
말들이 상한 딸기처럼 문드러져 나오십니까?
양손에 떡이십니까, 건망증에 섬망증?
막막하고 갑갑하십니까? 답답하고
캄캄하십니까? 곧 미칠 것
같은데, 같기만
하십니까?

여기를 클릭
하십시오

A Bubble's Birth 1

The I that makes urine out of beer
Is the I that forms bubbles out of urine
Inside my bubble I take off my clothes completely and stand
Venus pudica! Venus pudica!
Is the I that chews my hair strands
The I that sits on the edge of my throne on my toilet
Bending down to check the bottom of my feet, I wonder
Have I lived a life belittling to myself,
What do I look like entranced in this apprehension
When I ask if you can see
What do I look like in the eyes of the writhing furry bug
Stuck to the bottom of the bathtub
What do I even look like, can I even be seen

A Seashore's Tomb

The dogs wearing mid-summer fur with the white-shit filled cones at the tide riding mortuary with the love-infested ankles, the peculiar sailor's song heard at the landing with the mother who couldn't let the eye's thorn the throat's thorn the anus's thorn die at once, with the worn out corners of mother's pornography, the once canned regret recklessly pried open as a canned mouth full of red worms, with the old women who spread the smell of old fish to spare change, at the seaside eel restaurant, your right hand holding the scissors lightly chomp your left hand to eat, the fingers without fingernails dunked in the side plate for two hours

EX. 1) Carefully read the answers on the next page, and create proper questions out of your answers. (Describe in short answer form)

Question 01.
Question 02.
Question 03.
Question 04.
Question 05.
Question 06.
Question 07.
Question 08.
Question 09.
Question 10.
Question 11.
Question 12.
Question 13.
Question 14.
Question 15.
Question 16.

Answer 01. Crown of pubic hairs
Answer 02. After exceeding your excellent poem masturbation
Answer 03. Like pubes, poems that have waves and shine
Answer 04. Tapeworms that are born inside the intestines and die inside the intestines
Answer 05. Dirtily unfair and dirtily unfortunate witness
Answer 06. Will not go past 1.8 minutes
Answer 07. Go crazy if you have, go even more crazy if you don't
Answer 08. A fly agaric, amanita virosa, the coprinus atramentarius rotting up to the end of the tongue
Answer 09. A maggot on the tongue
Answer 10. The dog chewing gum in Eden
Answer 11. *Appendix with formulas for rudimentary familial relations*
Answer 12. Can use the welcome mat laid out at the gates of hell
Answer 13. If life changes then the motivation for derangement also changes
Answer 14. The mixed penis mayonnaise meal set
Answer 15. The yellow yolk only egg
Answer 16. Fallayavada (팔라야바다[5])

---

[5] This is the title of an installation by the artist Bahc Yiso

EX. 1) 옆 페이지의 정답을 잘 읽고, 그 정답에 적절한 질문을 작성하시오(주관식 서술형)

질문 01
질문 02
질문 03
질문 04
질문 05
질문 06
질문 07
질문 08
질문 09
질문 10
질문 11
질문 12
질문 13
질문 14
질문 15
질문 16

정답 1. 터럭 면류관
정답 2. 수음을 능가하므로
정답 3. 거웃처럼 윤기와 웨이브가 있는 시
정답 4. 내장 속에서 태어나 내장 속에서 죽는 촌충류
정답 5. 더럽게 불리한 더럽게 불길한 증인
정답 6. 1.8분을 넘기지 않는다
정답 7. 있으면 미친다, 없으면 더 미친다
정답 8. 광대버섯, 독우산광대버섯, 혓바닥까지 썩은 두엄먹물버섯들
정답 9. 혓바닥 위의 구더기
정답 10. 낙원의 개 껌
정답 11. 친족의 기본 구조에 달린 수학적 부록
정답 12. 지옥의 현관에 까는 환영 매트로 쓸 수 있다
정답 13. 인생이 변하면 착란의 모티브도 변하므로
정답 14. 마요네즈에 버무린 한 세트의 성기
정답 15. 노른자위뿐인 달걀
정답 16. 팔라야바다(*Fallayavada*)

Jangchung's King-size Pork Feet

You go away, even though I cut the ankle

Even though I boil the ankles!

You cut your own feet to
Not come back again

Over there, excuse me

Me.

You pigs winding up your dicks and leaving

Those Cats!

Those cats! Wrapping their four legs around the rolling tires! Those bright cats! Rolling, their haunches squeezed the tires! Those crashing cats! Carelessly tossing fur, tossing bone marrow and tossing intestines! Those cunning cats! Don't even have an inkling of thought to release their haunches! Those sweet cats. While rolling and coaxing and licking, run along with the tire! Those layered cats! Awaken like peeled notebook pages from the melted asphalt during a heat wave! Those sylphlike cats! Exhaust themselves from stretching! Those cats! Slightly open their bright yellow eyes and groom their broken toenails!

Star-Shining-Night

Teeth all falling out kind of night star shining kind of night pubic hair all

Falling out kind of night star shining kind of night

The crown of the head smack smack splitting open kind of night

Star shining kind of night shadows not appearing kind of night star shining kind of night

Night without secrets kind of night star shining kind of night

Without apparitions kind of night star shining kind of night

When the glass-like virgins return to glass kind of night star shining kind of night

When the whole armpit catches on fire, the lovers fly away kind of night

A sky held up by the flesh of the firework's blaze and gigantic neon coconut fruits

Fully bloom on the neon palm tree kind of night

Just a Moment

Please wait for
Just a moment

I'm in the middle of an arousal strut

Not the walk of shame
but the arousal strut
You don't have to be suspicious of their eyes

Yes, exactly that
Arousal strut
That's right

Just a moment, please wait

II

Vaseline Symphony

What I love
The big dipper's eighth star

What I love
The Chupa Chups that create holes in my tongue

What I love
The cat that catches and shreds apart the morning bird apart

What I love
The blood sucking cosmos and the lips that illuminate

What I love
The odalisque that's about to fart right now

What I love
The appetizing bomb inserted into the rectum

What I love
The jujube struck by lightning opened by the jujube tree to be struck by lightning

What I love
Your face that's just been bitten by a snake, dearest

Ark

I'm a seal sitting on a beach ball, if I hold my farts in
burps come out, but if I hold my burps in my farts come out,

Take a look at the seal, sitting arrogantly above the ark of the beach ball, like a pearl draped by a large thong ripening to settle,
The spectacle,
Above the beach ball!

You probably know but my nickname is erogenous zone, between
My ass and my thingy does anyone know what it's called?

These kinds of big thongs, amusingly, blood dryingly, ripening to settle,
Can't be found anywhere even early in the morning, oh my from where did the split occur, the buttocks early in the morning

The seals sit until their eyes falls out
Squeezing their asshole tightly, sitting on top of the slippery ark, *my hands*

They say is too small, to hide my lethal lure,

Even Now Something

While knocking on the door suddenly, the other door opens, once it's been opened, it is said it cannot be closed, be it night be it day, tongue and throat, dried and strangled, amorphophallus, the flower blooms in the brutal vast dark, frond, the insects grow plumply fat even though they're plumply fed pesticides, In [*The 21st Century Waste Digest*] they solicit my work, they push push, this rotting night, the dog, grew too large underneath the bed, the amor tightly bound between the upper and lower teeth, whenever a breath is taken the insides of the body are cut cut cut divided, more than anything, we cannot wait for more than thirty seconds, each time the spit is swallowed we can see the stuff that crawls out, without seeing it, phophallus, the no more than the sufficiently filthy life, this filthy life, without, amor, amorphophallus, even now there's something, that insufficiently needs something more, this disgusting thing, even more oleaginous, some things

Habituation (習)

I scratch my head until it bleeds. I insert long needles into my eyes to turn and look around. The extinct *aglao aglaonema commutatum* is part of the same species but *aglao aglaonema commutatuma* is not. Did extinction continuously span over a millions years? Over a hundred years? Did it happened just one morning? The creepy digital maggot crawls inside a digital sore. The radiant maggot wiggles on top of the retina. I shave off my eyebrows I shave off my pubes I yodel a song. The yodel song that never ends when it's supposed to. To memories for memories, to yodel songs for yodel songs, they avoid each other round and round. Gasping because the place they say you're supposed to reach cannot be reached, I fall asleep sprawled out recklessly having used a lethal technique. Darling, guzzle the stale water stuck in my skull, then go to India alone!

습(褶)

피가 날 때까지 머리를 긁어본다. 긴 바늘을 눈에 넣고 돌려본다. 멸종한 아글라오탐니온 테누이시뭄은 아글라오탐니온 비소이데스와 동종이지만 아글라오탐니온 수도비소이데스와는 동종이 아니다. 멸종은 백 만년에 걸쳐서 일어났을까? 백 년에 걸쳐 일어났을까? 하루아침에 일어났을까? 디지털 욕창에서 쑤물쑤물 디지털 구더기가 기어 나온다. 쑤물거리는 망막 위의 光 구더기. 눈썹을 밀고 불두덩을 밀고 요들송을 불러 본다. 끝나야 할 곳에서 끝나는 법이 없는 요들송. 기억이 기억을, 요들송이 요들송을 휙휙 피한다. 이르러야 한다는 곳에 이르는 법이 없는 헐떡임, 필살기를 헛 쓰고 쩍 벌리고 잠이 든다. 자기, 내 해골에 괴인 물까지 퍼 마셔, 마시고 천축(天竺)으로는 자기 혼자 가!

EX. 2) The insides (   ) of the poem below can be newly filled accordingly to your unique preferences

In the beginning
It was a filthy (   ) relationship

And then later it was obviously a much more filthy (   ) relationship

And finally it became an extremely filthy (   )
Relationship, for us

It became (   ) a filthiness that could only be completed through each other

To become more filth-y (   ) ier most filthy (   ) est it cannot become
That kind of filth (   )

Though it was
A banal (   ) filth
It too was (   ) a rare filth

EX. 2) 아래 시는 (   )속에 취향에 맞는 낱말을 넣어 새로 쓸 수 있습니다

처음에는
더러운(   ) 관계였다가

그런 다음에는 당연히 너무도 더러운(   ) 관계가

그리고 마침내는 극도로 더러운(   )
관계가 되어 갔어요, 우린

서로를 통해서만 완성되는 더러움(   )이었어요

더 더러워(   )질 래야 더 더러워(   )질 수가 없는
그런 더러움(   )

진부한
더러움(   )이었지만
진기한 더러움(   )이기도 했어요

Mantra

I am trying to become more yellow. I suppose the days in which scandals disappear do not exist in my life. Even though the beginning is insignificant The end is a prosperous vicious spell. Like cocks sequentially fraternizing like the dog who chases their tail I am trying to become tumescent. Like the decorational blowfish hanging inside the Japanese Restaurant this poison they say is the taste of being killed once. The second hand spins freely the minute hand spins freely the hour hand spins freely from the beginning to the end the bloodthirsty vagina unfolds. *The bloodthirsty vagina packed with violence* I am trying to lose my self. The snake cloud of smoke swallows the snake cloud of smoke slithering in front of my eyes I am trying harder to lose myself. If you see shit you know the asshole it came from. Do you think I am trying to concentrate after being coiled up I am trying to concentrate on the rising heated foul stench pieced together foul stench with foul stench I am trying more and most to become vividly yellow I am

The Traveler at the Beach

Even though you wash your eyes and look at the beach
The thing that washes ashore are a group of whales the size of anchovies
On the sandy beach a group of anchovies the size of whales
Turn around and sit pounding the rice cake pop
Pop pop pop pop pop pop pop after pounding
No matter how you look at it, this seal is that seal
Look you have to look even though you've washed your eyes
How is it that the right thing does not exist, look
How is it that the right thing cannot be seen, look
Even after washing and cleaning the bottom to see
How can you bite and shake this thing

Vexations

1
Just as a fly can can become itself on top of the dining table bewilderingly on the dining table a fly
It so surely happens that a Kim bewilderingly becomes a Kim

Bewilderingly

2
It so happens that no one looks for surname Kim however it so happens
Kim hides anyway
It so happens that there will be nothing else to do besides this

3
What should you think of when hanging by your neck, Kim will happen to ask
There will not be much to think about, Kim will happen to respond

4
As soon as Kim opens her mouth Kim will happen to have no ears
As soon as Kim perks up her ears Kim will happen to have no mouth
What Kim together with Kim can uniquely share will happen to be a state of ecstasy

It will be a unique ecstasy Kim can share together with Kim

5
It so happens Kim will laugh in a place where continuous laughter should not occur Kim will happen to cry in a place where crying should not occur Kim's laughter will happen to be a cry that irrespective of the type of cry cannot be cried Kim's cry will happen to be a laughter that irrespective of the type of laugh cannot be laughed They will always do it in places they should not have done it in Kim will always happen to squat in places they should not be squatting in It so happens the reason Kim themselves cannot understand Kim is because these are matters that should not be understood Kim increasingly will become a

laughingstock Kim will not been able to clench Kim's teeth
No matter how much they will try to clench their teeth their mouths will immediately open

6
From the moment Kim begins to stiffly stiffly strip themselves from Kim's awakening,
Kim will know that Kim's end has arrived, for Kim to Kim,
to Kim for Kim, to be extremely shear, to be extremely shear the deepest blue,
in that place Kim will start to gradually become filled with Kim, like the furnace of
a haunted house

7
In truth Kim will know not one thing about Kim during their lifetime Kim will keep
glancing at the back of Kim's head even asleep they will continue to glance during their lifetimes
Kim will be the kind of person who only shows Kim the back side of their head

8
Even though there's no being buried into oblivion or disappeared
Kim will not be able to be found or remembered

9
Nonetheless, just as stench is to shit Kim will be one with Kim
Nonetheless, Kim will speak to Kim with decorum
Nonetheless, every time Kim sees Kim they will vomit

Don't You Know When You Go You End up Sitting Down

Don't you know when you go you end up sitting down, don't you know when you sit you end up eating, don't you know you see the end only after vomiting—without leaving anything behind and eating everything up, don't you know the family dinner ends only when you ram your head into the dining table, don't you know the things that should take place will take place the way they should, don't you know the things I do is what dogs do in broad daylight, don't you know all spectacles are spectacles that cannot be believed, don't you know you have to tremble your legs as your chin is trembling, don't you know dearest I listen carefully to your words with my nostrils, don't you know it becomes complicated when the hole starts to laugh, don't you know there is a role for leftovers made by leftovers, don't you know you need more than the rest of your life just to speak gibberish, fearing you could gain the truth at this rate, you're becoming anxious that you could be born again a Latter-Day Saint at this rate, don't you know I alone cannot forget my own grace, don't you know I have never forgotten not a day not a time, because don't you know I am unable to fill my life with anything but this filth this language,

Feeding the Moon

I eat porridge with my dead mother's spoon

The one that has entered and left her dead mouth more than a thousand times

More than a thousand times in her dead mouth, the stainless steel spoon

I eat black porridge with the spoon she sucked

The moon rabbit grinds the iron mortar every night and

What was there was a mommy rabbit, say—ah

Mother ah—I spoon feed myself bite by bite

Putting the black porridge on my lips

And feed the black moon porridge like my mother

Funeral Bumper Car

I planted the
Elephant in the flowerpot
Into a hundred flowerpots, I divided
And planted them
In the garage I rode the submarine
With the backyard dog, until my hairs were tangled
In my throat, is there a way to
Not get off the roller coaster, ever
Is there a way to not get off
And die, the lunchbox bomb
That never once exploded on time, not once have
I wanted to drink
The gasoline and gulf down the fuming flames
With my lips, wherever I place my hands
Burn marks
Remained, inside the mousetrap
I lit the rat tail on fire,
Funeral bumper car, at the speed
Of 140, there I let my hands off
The steering wheel
Go,

운구(運柩)용 범퍼 카

코끼리를
화분에 심었어,
백 개의 화분에 나눠
심었어, 창고에서 뒷집 개와
잠수함을 탔어, 목구멍에 털이
엉겼어, 롤러 코스트에서
안 내리는 수는, 영영
안 내리고 죽는
수는 없나, 한 번도
제 시간에 터져 준 적이
없는 도시락
폭탄, 휘발유를
마시고 입으로 훌훌 불을 뿜고
싶었어, 손을 대는 곳
마다 불 탄 자국이
남았어, 쥐덫 속
의 쥐꼬리에 불을 붙였어,
운구용 범퍼 카, 시속
백사십의 핸들에서
손을
놓았어,

Your Mouth

The stitched on eyelids, with each strand of my hair, and with my pubic hair, The stitched on lips, however, cannot be stitched, chop chop chop the sound of the axe being fed, the sound of the flesh chewing flesh, the sound of bone breaking bones, cannot be stitched, the puddle of blood at your feet, the sound the fly makes splashing in the puddle, the flutter of the blue gold wings, cannot be stitched, the smell of your body without a body, cannot be stitched, cannot be stitched, your eyes filled with ash, cannot be stitched, your mouth filled with blood

Playing With Fireworks on the Moon 1

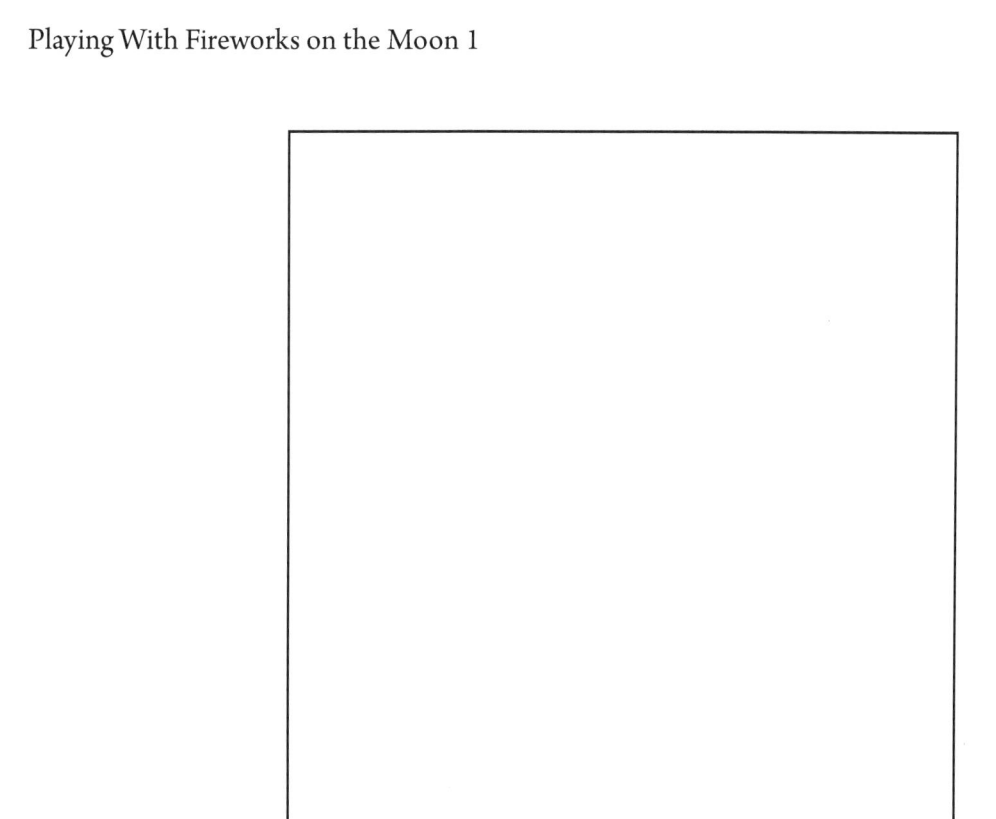

LOUISE BOURGEOIS, 1982. R. MAPPLETHORPE.

Playing With Fireworks on the Moon 2

Before the dawn rooster crows
I with the beauty of a demon
and lasciviousness like a demon
Cum three times exactly

Before the dawn rooster crows
I burn anything
Pitch black until my eyeballs are
Playing with fireworks on the moon

Before the dawn rooster crows
I lascivious like god
Put the pillow-size cock
On my side

Summer Icicle

It was a thing that drove me mad, that is

I was contained
Inside a large soap bubble
It was a thing that drove me mad

If you explode, you
Will already be dead

During that summer
When you straighten a crooked summer cock, it immediately crooks again
Over the roof
I threw the wisdom tooth pulled out of the asshole

After the blood water licks the entire roof and spills down
It's frozen by the heat wave
At the end of the eaves
Frozen over and frozen again
The icicle snaps
Breaking
Stuck to top of the naked foot, stuck

Tremblingly it shivered

Singing the national anthem into the asshole because

Till the fourth verse because
You were the first to sing it to me
Dearest

Day of Mourning

……….

Back then, when we boiled the seagulls only foam remained,
We discovered the taste of
This foam!

……….

Yup, it's the feeling of shoving your head into a large
Jar
Like having your head swiftly bitten off, again and again

…….

That's right, it will grow larger and larger inside the mouth, that candy
It'll get so big you won't be able to spit it out
That black candy, you can't spit it out
I'm sorry

………., please

Don't look at me so intently, with your eyes like pale oysters
Please, your genitals like pale oysters

………

Because we were so beautiful
We were, disgraced

After We Have Loved

We grill the meat after we have loved, and I will flip
My own meat, after we have loved, with legs shorter
Than I thought, with arms shorter than I thought,
After we have loved, how come, little by little there's no place to live,
How come little by little, there are no places to die,
After we have loved, with uvulas more crimson than I thought, after we have loved
With tongues more crimson than I thought, pi pi pie
Pie, brushing my teeth with the toothbrush used to clean the toilet, cleaning
The toilet with the toothbrush used to brush my teeth, what kind of end
Is this, what kind of end can be like this, after we have loved,
Up to the throat this love, like a shit house filled up to the brim,
After we have loved

Before You Came

Even after you have fallen asleep Bobo, your
Testicles don't know how to fall asleep
Slowly roll your eyes Bobo
I really didn't know I'd hear the sound
Of the eyes rolling Bobo

Before you came my sins had all
Been white, Bobo, white
Gluttony, white carnal desire steamed like laundry
The sins were white Bobo
The meat that touched my lips were all
White meat before you came

Any cat said to be a cat, all
Licked me, any flower petal
Said to be a flower petal, all took
And devoured me as if I were becoming
Falling snow

Rodeo

The father was a father for 8 seconds
The death was a death for 8 seconds
The romance was a romance for 8 seconds

The 8 seconds the fold between your fingers don't stick together stick
The 8 seconds you apply lipstick in the bathroom
The 8 seconds you can't get it over with anyone
The 8 seconds you can't get it over even with yourself

The 8 seconds before sleep pours over like starchy syrup

Postscript

Please do not roll up your sleeves, do not try to glimpse the subplot, it cannot be laughed off.
Even if you roll up your sleeves, please do not insert your forearms so
Knee deep into the multivocal sext. No matter if you fucked with lubricant

Even if you did, no matter if it's sex or murder it's one and the same, this kind of sexual practice this kind of aesthetic practice, it's both a mutual execution and your own execution, and the coloanal surgeons and doctors have repeatedly warned us, either could rupture the internal organs.

Whether it's poetic compulsion or sexual compulsion it's one and the same,
The nylon string attached to this poetry volume is used for masturbating or is only used for self-injury. There's nowhere

For it to be used. Old folks are too old to read, young folk too young to read, this poem, the 00:50 Daejeon Runaway Train, is merely the absurdist work of an **avant-garde** past its prime you like to sing anyway. So there's that.

Why bother heading towards Mokpo's end? Doggedly riding the ho-hum moving train, while cutting again the cut gullet

A Very Special Bouquet

I suddenly missed, continuously missed the
moment, go, I was supposed to scream,
Damn, go and eat shit!
My first speech is also
My last speech

With my back turned as it is, I made an appearance and then with my back turned as it is
My role was to exit the stage
Before my
One and only
Speech ends

The bouquet I received

Is a very very special bouquet
A very special person
Specially delivered
Specially

The bouquet
A bouquet of sphincter, the hole through which I pass you dear
Is the same hole through which you pass me
Even though I am suddenly

Continuously missing
The moment, I am supposed to scream

Magna Carta
    —If only you could proclaim and cry out at the same time

I have the right to be rotting from the morning and
Also have the right to start the day by vomiting
I have the right to be incompetent everyday and
Also have the right to not understand what everyone else does
The right to ride the ark of the black concrete and dream of disastrous floods every night
The right to dream every night of a pile of shit hovering softly above my head
The right to not recognize even my parents and to enjoy my mother's obituary
Just for only five minutes
The right to shake my legs while wailing and the right to be whistling
Behind the screen
I have the right to always correct panis angelicus
To penis angelicus and
Also have the right to masturbate until I stop breathing
The right to masturbate while I stop breathing
I have the right to no longer be curious about the future and
Also have the right to play the chopstick marching song for thirty years, the right
To play that song until I bleed
I have the right to think about sweet flesh while having sweet meat
In my mouth and
Also the right to start it complicatedly and see it end awkwardly
The right to force the moan to make it end
I have the right to tighten my anus five hundred times a day to try and change my life
Also the right to hold out the axe I trust on the top of my foot
I have the right to further blind my blind eye
And most importantly the right to use chopsticks with my feet
Like the right of a pigeon to brazenly shit on the crown of my head
In a grand park

III

Bruise

The late summer peaches will
Bruise carelessly, their rotting an indication
of never having learned to rot

Like when calming the mad dogs with the
Fingers used to calm my genitals like when calming
The mad dogs my corpse calms

Wherever my fingers reach, black bruises
Remain and from the black bruises, short
Soft fur sprouts

Plum

The plums are being peeled with my mother's fingernails

As if they were eyelids, beneath the curling drying skin

The red black plum opens their eyes on their own

Entangled with blood veins and lifting their red eyes

Once opened, daughter daughter my only daughter mother

After feeding me plums my mother places it in my bite

The sclera wet with evil blood

After the plums are peeled with my mother's fingernails, only daughter

My sweet daughter now peeling the blood plums

Together
	—To K, an Esteemed Friend

Together with the blank sheets to exfoliate until blood comes out
Together with the slaughtered animals above the blank sheets
Together with the horns and intestines

Together with the bone-cutting romance together with the bone-cutting moan

Together
With the days like dog hair's with adultery like dog hairs
With adulteress deeds

Together with chills

Together with goose eggs boiled in piss
Together with the watermelon-like seminal vesicles of the aroused goats
Together with god, he who loves me

Loves me till the cock falls out
Little me
With the god that bites and sucks, together with

"I say that the true artist seer, the heavenly fool who can and does produce beauty, is mainly dazzled to death by his own scruples, the blinding shapes and colors of his own human conscience."

—J.D. Salinger

Fish Cake Dumplings

I can't fall asleep, I take a digestive, the sound of my brain barking, the sound of my heart barking, the sound of my womb barking, I take a digestive, thirty-four times the doorbell, rings and halts, the digestive, when your mother was eating her shit where were you, I was actually right next to her, eat, the elderly mother's, living bubble, living cow shit, intention, it was not, but it was not not the intention, the digestive, the blood stain that did not even appear, becomes all the more crimson, becomes all the more scattered, when was the last time you took the digestives, I want to eat, the digestives, the fish cake dumplings, the kind that gently melts my tongue,

Snuff, Snuff, Snuff

You see, the video that I really want to watch is a snuff, a snuff film in which you appear as the main character. You die and you die but it's not like you're dead, right dear? Even after you're dead, you want to die more, right? More more more more, you want to die more.

That's the killer, right? This excessive struggle, during the climax you peak peak peak peak flatline, this excessive ecstasy, the excessive smoke flowing out of the opening. Wow dearest, the thing that's only supposed to come once, has come a hundred times over!

That which is not love it is not, that which is not instantaneous death it is not, in other words, life, what has come a hundred times. What should we eat, should we eat something, what should we be eating, lunch? While the steam from the anus cools down, a complimentary raw liver and lung arrives.

Dancing dancing you take the throat but stop. when I. say freeze. So when will the frozen throat be taken away completely. The wax skull in the flower pot hiccups every three minutes. The wax skull in the flower pot requests water every three minutes.

스너프, 스너프, 스너프

있지, 내가 진짜 보고 싶은 비디오는 스너프야, 당신이 주인공으로 등장하는 스너프. 죽어도 죽어도 죽은 것 같지가 않지, 당신? 죽은 뒤에도 더, 죽고 싶지? 더 더 더 더 죽고 싶어

죽겠지? 이 과도한 몸부림, 클라이맥스에서 픽 픽 픽 픽 김이 빠지는, 이 과도한 황홀경, 질구에서 흘러나오는 이 과도한 연기. 여보, 한번만 와야 하는 것이 골백번, 와!

골백번 오는, 사랑이 아닌 것은 아닌, 즉사(卽死)가 아닌 것은 아닌, 즉, 생(生). 뭐 먹지, 점심? 뭐 먹을까 뭘 먹어야 하지, 점심? 똥구멍의 김이 식어 가는 동안, 서비스로 나오는 생간과 허파.

즐겁게 멱을 따다가 그대로 멈.춰.라. 멈춘 멱은 언제 마저 따게 되나. 삼 분마다 딸꾹질을 하는 화분 속의 촉루(髑髏), 삼 분마다 물을 청하는 화분 속의 촉루.

Liaison

I am eating the fig; scarily, so voraciously it disappears as soon as it touches my mouth

The fig's lips suckily sticks to my mouth

The fig towards me, the lips touching the other lips

I make slurping sounds suckling the fig

They are so sweet my eyes can't open

Dear child of a ghost inside the fig's mouth, dear child of ghosts

The lips of the master spirit slurpily sticks to my mouth

Facing mother ghost our lips lock, the lips touching the other lips

Mother ghost makes slurping sounds suckling me out

밀통(密通)

무화과를 먹는다 입대기 무섭게

입에 쩍쩍 달라붙는 무화과의 입

입에 입을 맞대고 무화과는 나를

나는 무화과를 쭉쭉 소리 내어 빤다

너무 달콤해서 눈이 떠지지 않는

무화과의 입 속 鬼子야 鬼子야

입에 짝짝 들러붙는 몸주의 입

입에 입을 맞대고 나는 鬼母를

鬼母는 나를 쭉쭉 소리 내어 빤다

Mantis

It was
The mantis, crunch crunch
The lustful lower jaw chews
The back of my head, it was
The old mother, with morning sickness for twenty-four hours
A mouth that's not the mouth
With the jet-black smile
The mantis'
Day has five nights
Winding my waist with its nothing-but-bones-left legs five times a day and
Becomes a corpse on top of my stomach
Please tumble and stay away, you!
More than death
Biting with a plentiful laugh
Bit by bit forcefully it put me into a plentiful
Crotch, plentiful priming water, the old mother
It was, a mantis
It was,

The Portrait of Princess Bonaparte

—yourdaddyhockedseedsintomywomblikesalivathatisall

—hewasburnedalivebuttheysaidcauseofdeathisconstipation

—likeatoiletthegodhasnoquestions

—youandIarecamelswiththecurveoffourkneesseveredaswesitontopofourgravesthecamels

—Iwonderwhyanyonewouldprotectahumanlikemaggot

—onlymyrighthandwantstotrulydoitwithme

—ponderingwhytheydemandsexthattearseventhoughit'sdry

—thankyouIreceivedthepoetrybookyousentmethepoemsaretrulygreatshouldIsayitfeltlikeIwipedmyasswithaspiderweb

—thatmyfatherjusttookhislastbreathwhydoIhavetoknowthis

—isthereawaytonotgetofftherollercoasteryetnotdie

—thatbastardentertainedmomwithspermit'sanidealfantasybetweenamotherandsondon'tyouthink

—*thenightbirthsthesonsthenighteats*Ibirththesonsleat

—theyawnthatrescuesfromthetearsofreachingclimax

—EachtimeIuncorkthebottlewithanopenerIgetthefeelingthatI'mpoppingsomeone'seyesout

—Suchisanappearancelikeducksbeingculled,runningpell-mell,underthecloakedsnow

—Isawinmydreamsthegoldpig'sneckwascleavedassoonasitmorphedintomyteacher

—Ismiledforthefirsttimeinsevenyears

—

—

Someone, Again

Who is once again gassing these bubbly water bubbles
It's the first I've seen of such rotten water and underneath it
I am here...... who is smiling with a mouth full of worms,
rotten rats rotten snakes rotten dogs rotten umbilical cords
until the uvula, who is full of mud *I am here......* smiling
With artificial teeth bigger than the face of this one night
Who is once again **splashing** inside my body! Who throws
This body

A Very Very Blue Meridian

After I bloom the morning glory and feed them my tongue after I bloom the morning glory and feed them my ears after I bloom the morning glory and feed them my gallbladder the morning glory does the morning is, my body does my body is wrapped to die and coiled die die get on the ride woohoo jump right on and jump around, my vines strangle my neck to die die die gripping tightly to the morning glory's meridian, barely I climb over, the morning glory is the morning does barely, submits to the morning glory entirely I am I do submit myself entirely to the morning glory trembling I shake off my eyelids shaking the morning glory sucks me up the morning glory's cupules the morning glory's placenta is without blood and tears but nevertheless is very blue

Shadow Spider (Yaginumia Sia)

As if she were dead my mother waits
As if she were to die she waits

With sunlight I attempt to burn my mother's left eye using the convex lens

From my mother's eye a stream of smoke floods
She holds her breath, my mother

As if to kill, as if dead my mother waits

Gathering more sunlight I attempt to finish burning the remaining eye

From my mother's eye a strand of yellowish urine flows, her lips
Don't even move slightly, my mother

From her toothless greyish gums to the back of her tongue
Steadily

She devours her mouth, my mother

A Bubble's Birth 2

Why have I been reborn
In the half-filled beer mug
Of the bubble, the bubble does bite
Of the burp, the burp does bite a

Singularly extremely portioned figure a
Singularly exceedingly portioned figure
Of the lips, the lip does bite
Of the vagina, the vagina does bite
To be reborn for what reason

For what reason to finish in one day
Singularly anxiously in *layers*
As I gather my piss and drink it
I *anxiously* write poetry
So well I who is chronically ill

For what would be good to drink
After I drink my piss, again
For what would be good to drink
After drinking even the bubbles again

Her Specialty, Doorbell

Ring ring the doorbell rings
Damp like the damp night air
Rings in the antique inn
I go to greet the guest who stays the long night
Roundworm like fingers the pale white guest
Ring ring the buzzer rings
The bed bug blood stained bed bug blood stain muted
I go to tuck in the guest who stays the long night
In this nose-less night
I go to sing that incredibly creepy
Incredibly obscene old song
My golden specialty

Her Specialty, Fox Tail

Hourly room rate twenty-five dollars, overnight room rate thirty dollars
The leather of a flabby hog was plastered onto the walls in the room
I did not want you to touch even a strand of hair on my head
Instead I just wanted you to sleep, always
Waking up in pivotal moments, in every
Pivotal dream, I do not know whether I was a man dreaming, I was a butterfly
Or I am now a butterfly, dreaming I am having sex with ghosts
It's June Honorary Third-day, please feast on those orangutan lips
I will order and eat duruchigi in front of the TV
Spreading out the newspaper that rustles
And placing on top of my spoon the snot of
The ghost that was casually picked on the one night
A thousand water fleas died and left
The Musty Riverside Inn oh yo yo
On top of my hand Honorary Oh Yo Yo's fox tail bubbles
Fox tail
Flowing even from the nostrils

Prelude

Inside the toilet
If you start seeing a mantis then, if you start having a relationship
With a mantis and can confide in them then, in broad daylight
If my dog starts to insidiously bark at me
Then, you wouldn't even know it was there
The not knowing,
If every time you open the door
It starts to be outside the door then, that would disgust me like my previous wife
And if by coincidence we run into and can't
Avoid each other
If we start to run into each other then, if you start to step on shit on the escalator
Then, only my feet will be slippery-shit-ish
If my feet starts to be shit-ish then, if the hand starts to leave behind
A burn imprint wherever
The hand touches then, if on the fingernails toenails start to grow
Then, if ominous articles inside the bag prompt
The flower to
Bloom then, the flower
Without one petal will sparkle sparkle
If it starts to bloom then,
Even without a face
Blatantly
If it starts to stare then,

Buck Teeth

The world's most protracted buck teeth
You, I've taken a liking to you dear, close to my face
Carp carp you who makes smoke donuts dear
Lean on the donut and make it clap clap
Dear I've taken a liking to you, I've really taken a liking to you
You who no one has seen you
Why call out to someone who's turned around and is going
Carrying the smell of rotten eggs, calling out always
Stopping me in my tracks I've taken a liking to you, I've really taken a liking to you
On one side the testicles have been frozen orange on the other side the testicles
Rotten orange pop so blackened your fingers can easily penetrate pop
Even though clank it's frozen still
Drip I melt, I've taken a liking to you dear, lips
Puckered like an asshole carp carp
You make the smoke donuts fly, the world's most
Protracted buck teeth you, I've taken a liking to you dear

(Whisperingly)

it's me, dear, the genitals of Buddha's boundless mercy of your dreams, it's me, me dear, the one you feed your fingers to when it's night every night, gradually rubbing more saliva to eat, it's me, the octopus hole not any hole of anyone else, it's me, me, who faithfully enters nirvana with my hand, guffawing at nirvana's threshold, the guffawing vagina, it's me, dear, the genitals of universal compassion in your dreams, the one you have to take your eyes off to but can't take your eyes off, the one you have to spin but cannot spin, it's me, me, the one who perfectly matches with you dear eye-to-eye it's you dear.

(속삭이듯이)

나야, 당신이 꿈꾸는 대자대비(大慈大悲)한 음부, 나야, 나, 밤이면 밤마다 당신이 손가락을 먹이는, 점점 더 많은 침을 발라 가며 먹이는, 나야, 그 누구의 구멍도 아닌 낙지구멍, 나야, 나, 꼬박꼬박 내 손으로 열반에 드는, 열반의 문지방에서 너털웃음 치는, 너털웃음 치는 음문, 나야, 당신이 꿈꾸는 동체대비(同體大悲)한 음부, 눈을 떼려야 뗄 수가 없는, 돌리려야 돌릴 수가 없는, 나야, 나, 당신과 눈이 딱딱 마주치는 당신이야,

5 Minutes Have Passed

5 minutes since the bird's shit dropped into the fedora

5 minutes since you suddenly stood up

5 minutes since mother couldn't stick out her tongue at me

5 minutes since the past has passed

5 minutes since you abandoned the dead leaf

5 minutes since you started believing in god

5 minutes since I've become a new me

5 minutes since my hair went up in flames

5 minutes since I appeared in this dream

Pieta Signore

I lick
The mirror
With my tongue

Inside the mirror I lick god

Tongue to tongue they meet and
I, also face
God
Who graciously licks me

Put the nail hammered tongue on the nail hammered tongue hammered and

Of lustful father
Of lustful mother
And of the lustful son of

God

Ver. 1 Ignite

The dog barks even though my hair catches fire
The dog barks even though my lips catch fire
The dog barks even though the fire now spreads inside setting my tongue ablaze
The dog barks even though my blazing hair rolls down to my feet
The dog barks even though lava flows out of my belly button
The dog barks even though the burning gravel rolls into my blood vessels
The dog barks even though white steam comes out of my screams
The dog barks even though the fire now spreads setting my screams ablaze
The dog barks even though my flesh stock becomes so hot it flutter flutters leaps away

Filthy Love

A pile of birds was stacked on top of a board
The grinder was grinding as the sound was completely killed
It was a thrown out bird with gouged out eyes
The cold oil was flowing down the edge
I drank lukewarm lubricant leaning on a toxic waste barrel
The dirtiest thing that could happen to me has not yet happened
I clenched the wood shavings firmly with my anus
The wood shavings were pushed out of the sockets of
The gouged out eyes

If you only spin
The corner
You arrive at the end of the waste facility *in filthy love*
going on the filthy love way, the moon

Came up
Rising crimson red

Like blood stained
Iron

The Dragon Door's Aftertaste

it was a taste that allowed everything to be forgiven, it was a scary lever,

just by a whiff it was a vagina that made you feel alive, just by its whiff

it was a question that made you go crazy, without knowing how to tire

it was a chorus that was repeated, without knowing how to tire it was

the anal of the chorus, it was crossing the rotten suspension bridge

while laughing, it was a pocket watch swinging on top of the rotten bridge,

it was a wet dream of a life so hard snow white hair three thousand meters long,

it was my body the dragon door's accommodation, behind the filth it was the delight,

behind the filth it was the dragon door, the dragon door's aftertaste

Returning Home

Oh sweet ass
Oh sweet ass

Under the bed breaking wind oh sweet ass

Remove the ear remove the penis and only the voice remains oh sweet ass
Remove the ear remove the penis and only the smell remains oh my sweet ass

Let's go let's go hurry let's go
Dead father with his butthole opened

Hurry up

Epilogue

You don't know how old you are. You are so old your leather has all been peeled away and your bones are protruding out of your skin. *On the deformed breasts you pin on a penis, you old woman bastard.* You don't know if you are an old person or an old woman. Your enemy has already forgotten you. Even your penis has forgotten you. You are a fictional cloud floating above in a fictional sky. You are left hovering in the air still floating above the stage after the magician leaves.

ACKNOWLEDGEMENTS

We are grateful to Kim Eon Hee's generosity throughout the process,
for Don Mee Choi who introduced us to the poet,
the Literature Translation Institute of Korea for supporting us through a grant,
our designer Sarah Gzemski and Noemi Press,
and for Carmen Giménez Smith's incisive editorial guidance.
We also thank early readers of the translations:
our loves, friends, comrades.

This book is dedicated to the relationships in our lives: our ongoing,
stabilizing, difficult and fractured relationships. Thank you for helping us
understand the world in more meaningful ways.

Kim Eon Hee was born in 1953 in Jinju, Gyeongsang Province. She is the author of five volumes of poetry. Her first collection *Modern Ars Poetica* was published in 1989. Followed by, *Trunk, The Girl who Sleeps Under a Withering Cherry Tree, Unexpected Response*, and her latest from 2016 *The Man I Miss*. First published in 2011, *Have You Been Feeling Blue These Days?*, is her fourth poetry collection, and the first of her books' to be translated into English.

Sung Gi Kim is an award-winning journalist and photographer who writes about Asian affairs with a focus on the Korean Peninsula. He is a Seoul correspondent and producer for Thomson Reuters. He was part of a team that produced a documentary on South Korea's education system, which won silver at the 2016 New York Festivals. His work has been published in *The Sunday Times, Australian Broadcasting Corporation, Nikkei Asian Review* and *United Press International*.

Eunsong Kim is an Assistant Professor in the Department of English at Northeastern University. Her book project in progress, *The Politics of Collecting: Property, Race & Aesthetic Formations* considers how legal conceptions of racialized property become foundational to avant-garde and modern understandings of innovation in the arts. She co-founded the arts forum, *contemporary*, a platform supported by the Andy Warhol Art Writers Grant Program. Her essays have appeared in: *Lateral: Journal of the Cultural Studies Association, Journal of Critical Library and Information Studies*, and in the book anthologies, *Poetics of Social Engagement* and *Reading Modernism with Machines*. Her poetry has appeared in the *Brooklyn Magazine, The Iowa Review, Minnesota Review*, and *West Branch* amongst others. Her first book of poetry, *gospel of regicide*, was published by Noemi Press in 2017.